THE PRAYING ATHLETE™
QUOTE BOOK

ALL 8 VOLUMES

BY ROBERT B. WALKER

Copyright © 2019 by Robert B. Walker

All rights reserved. No part of this publication may be reproduced, stored in a retrieval system, or transmitted in any form or by any means — electronic, mechanical, photocopy, recording, or any other — except for brief quotation in printed reviews, without the prior written permission of the publisher.

Unless otherwise indicated, Scripture quotations in this book are taken from The Holy Bible, *New International Version®, NIV®*. Copyright © 1973, 1978, 1984, 2011 by Biblica, Inc.™ Used by permission. All rights reserved worldwide.

Published by The Core Media Group, Inc., P.O. Box 2037, Indian Trail, NC 28079.

Cover & Interior Design: Ashlyn Helms

Printed in the United States of America.

TABLE OF CONTENTS

VOL 1 PLAYING THE GAME 05

VOL 2 TEAM WORK 37

VOL 3 GROWTH & PREPARATION
FOR THE FUTURE 69

VOL 4 KEEPING THE RIGHT MENTALITY 101

VOL 5 STAYING MOTIVATED 133

VOL 6 PERSONAL ACCOUNTABILITY 165

VOL 7 LIVING LIFE PT. 1 197

VOL 8 LIVING LIFE PT. 2 229

VOL 1
PLAYING THE GAME

THE PRAYING ATHLETE

Many times in life we have to be patient and let the game melt into our focus. You cannot force something that is not there. Power versus Power only makes for a collision. Find the right window and then burst through it with excitement and power to find the green grass, daylight, and celebration—the End Zone!

"A hot-tempered person stirs up conflict, but the one who is patient calms a quarrel."
Proverbs 15:18

_____
_____
_____
_____

One day, one game or one play, whether good or bad, shall never define my heart or my God-given talents. I press on, prepare and plan for the next game, the next play, and the next day. This is what I can control: the preparation and focus on what is ahead. This day is done and cannot be changed. I have embraced what I learned today and now it is behind me.

"Not that I have already obtained all this, or have already arrived at my goal, but I press on to take hold of that for which Christ Jesus took hold of me."
Philippians 3:12

_____
_____
_____
_____

People look up to athletes as role models. Use your talents as a platform to promote the One who gifted you.

"Whoever claims to live in him must live as Jesus did."
1 John 2:6

Eight ways to build confidence in competition:
1- Stay focused on what you want to achieve.
2- Train with a plan.
3- Play with passion.
4- Fight to win, not survive.
5- Be purposeful in your goals and direction.
6- Master your skills.
7- Overcome distractions.
8- Do nothing to delay your dream.

"For the Lord will at your side and will keep your foot from being snared."
Proverbs 3:26

_____
_____
_____
_____

There is a difference between winning championships and being a champion.

"For everyone born of God overcomes the world. This is the victory that has overcome the world, even our faith. Who is it that overcomes the world? Only the one who believes that Jesus is the Son of God."
1 John 5:4-5

If you think you will have a great season, you are probably right. If you think you will have bad season, you are probably right. What we believe dictates the reality we live in.

"Truly I tell you, if anyone says to this mountain, 'Go throw yourself into the sea,' and does not doubt in their heart but believes that what they say will happen, it will be done for them."
Mark 11:23

THE PRAYING ATHLETE

Step toward your inner self to find peace of mind and confidence to win.

"You will keep in perfect peace those whose minds are steadfast, because they trust in you."
Isaiah 26:3

_____
_____
_____
_____

Perfection will always be paralyzing, and limit your potential, until you realize perfection is really pressing toward a goal that can only be chased and never caught.

"Indeed, there is no one on earth who is righteous, no one who does what is right and never sins."
Ecclesiastes 7:20

As you engage yourself in game day remember this: OPEN, O = ONE, P= PLAY, E=EXECUTE, N= NOW. Write it down so you can see it and then believe in it. "OPEN" is a focus factor to achieve success on the field. If you stay focused on what happened during the play before, or what could happen next, or how you are feeling, you have lost your ability to excel on the current play. Focus on the current play, which is 3-6 seconds. Embrace "OPEN" and it will change your mental performance to enhance your physical performance.

"For if the willingness is there, the gift is acceptable according to what one has, not according to what one does not have."
2 Corinthians 8:12

_____
_____
_____
_____

Sometimes there is a voice telling you to quit now and avoid failure, and telling you that success is impossible. Don't listen to this voice. If you put everything into what you are striving for, you could make it. Quitting before you try will bring a heavy heart of dissatisfaction, and you will always find yourself asking the question, "What if...?" Don't ever doubt yourself. Stay the course. Pray, Work, Believe, and Be Confident! Go out and play the game with passion and desire.

"Let us not become weary in doing good, for at the proper time we will reap a harvest if we do not give up."
Galatians 6:9

_____
_____
_____
_____

THE PRAYING ATHLETE

Play each game as if it is your first and your last. You will find gratitude that you can play and sadness that the game will soon be over. This combination creates enthusiasm for the moment.

"And whatever you do, whether in word or deed, do it all in the name of the Lord Jesus, giving thanks to God the Father through him."
Colossians 3:17

_____
_____
_____
_____

Passion will lead you to success. Lack of passion leads you nowhere. Bring passion for the game you love.

Whatever you do, work at it with all your heart, as working for the Lord, not for human masters."
Colossians 3:23

THE PRAYING ATHLETE

Don't pray for a win, thank God for a chance to compete.

"Give thanks in all circumstances; for this is God's will for you in Christ Jesus."
1 Thessalonians 5:18

Maintain a high level of confidence in your skill set. Never allow others to take what you already own. It is your confidence, not theirs, so keep ownership of it.

"So do not throw away your confidence; it will be richly rewarded. You need to persevere so that when you have done the will of God, you will receive what he has promised."
Hebrews 10:35-36

**Building confidence is a
two-step process:
1- Stop thinking.
2- Start Believing.**

"Therefore I tell you, whatever you ask for in prayer, believe that you have received it, and it will be yours."
Mark 11:24

VOL 1 PLAYING THE GAME

Play for the love you have for the game, not for the love the game gives you.

"For where your treasure is, there your heart will be also."
Matthew 6:21

Work your wins into existence.

"A sluggard's appetite is never filled,
but the desires of the diligent
are fully satisfied."
Proverbs 13:4

VOL 1 PLAYING THE GAME

Winning today is much more important than winning yesterday.

"The Lord has done it this very day; let us rejoice today and be glad."
Psalm 118:24

Always play for the outcome: the love of the game, the passion to do what you love. Never play for the income. If you play for the outcome, the income will surpass your own thoughts and dreams.

"Do you not know that in a race all the runners run, but only one gets the prize? Run in such a way as to get the prize. Everyone who competes in the games goes into strict training. They do it to get a crown that will not last, but we do it to get a crown that will last forever."
1 Corinthians 9:24-25

Your skill set is an art, but an artist who does not perform may lose those skills. Practice often.

"Watch out that you do not lose what we have worked for, but that you may be rewarded fully."
2 John 1:8

THE PRAYING ATHLETE

Difficult practices make for easy games.

"Blessed is the one who perseveres under trial because, having stood the test, that person will receive the crown of life that the Lord has promised to those who love him."
James 1:12

Be focused on what you can do for the game and the game will reward you.

"Commit to the Lord whatever you do, and he will establish your plans."
Proverbs 16:3

Don't dwell on the wins and losses of the past. The most important game of your life is the next one.

"Forget the former things; do not dwell on the past. See, I am doing a new thing! Now it springs up; do you not perceive it? I am making a way in the wilderness and streams in the wasteland."
Isaiah 43:18-19

Often times we wish we could retake our last shot and give it another try. The game is unforgiving, but that doesn't mean you have to be as well. Always give people a second chance.

"Be kind and compassionate to one another, forgiving one another, just as in Christ God forgave you."
Ephesians 4:32

THE PRAYING ATHLETE

You can undo some things in life, but you cannot undo the scoreboard.

"For all have sinned and fall short of the glory of God."
Romans 3:23

VOL 1 PLAYING THE GAME

If the player you are is not the player you want to be, stop making excuses and work toward who you want to become.

"Blessed is the one who does not walk in step with the wicked or stand in the way that sinners take or sit in the company of mockers, but whose delight is in the law of the Lord, and who meditates on his law day and night."
Psalm 1:1-2

_____
_____
_____
_____

If your goal is only to be better than the next guy, you are limiting yourself from what you can achieve.

"If anyone thinks they are something they are not, they deceive themselves. Each one should test their own actions. Then they can take pride in themselves alone, without comparing themselves to someone else, for each one should carry their own load."
Galatians 6:3-5

**Getting there is hard.
Staying there is harder.
Being there is a blessing.**

"But as for you, be strong and do not
give up, for your work will
be rewarded."
2 Chronicles 15:7

THE PRAYING ATHLETE

A comeback is dependent on you.

"Now to him who is able to do immeasurably more than all we ask or imagine, according to his power that is at work within us..."
Ephesians 3:20

_____
_____
_____
_____

Challenges will come and go; when they come, just press on. The storm always ends.

"I consider that our present sufferings are not worth comparing with the glory that will be revealed in us."
Romans 8:18

VOL 2 TEAM WORK

Be the teammate you seek in your peers, and you will build a better team.

"Each of you should use whatever gift you have received to serve others, as faithful stewards of God's grace in its various forms."
1 Peter 4:10

You can prolong your career by putting the right people on your team.

"As iron sharpens iron, so one person sharpens another."
Proverbs 27:17

THE PRAYING ATHLETE

To be aligned with your team means you must be totally committed to what is best for your team, not yourself.

"Do to others as you would
have them do to you."
Luke 6:31

_____
_____
_____
_____

Pleasing your coach cannot be your focus. The purpose of the team should be your focus.

"For even the Son of Man did not come to be served, but to serve, and to give his life as a ransom for many."
Mark 10:45

Every team is under construction daily. Be patient.

"But if we hope for what we do not yet have, we wait for it patiently."
Romans 8:25

Encourage your teammates, and you will be encouraged.

"Do not let any unwholesome talk come out of your mouths, but only what is helpful for building others up according to their needs, that it may benefit those who listen."
Ephesians 4:29

THE PRAYING ATHLETE

Toss out all your team's emotional garbage and start fresh today.

"But now, by dying to what once bound us, we have been released from the law so that we serve in the new way of the Spirit, and not in the old way of the written code."
Romans 7:6

VOL 2 TEAMWORK

Live through the struggles and victories with your teammates—teamwork is a journey of endurance.

"From him the whole body, joined and held together by every supporting ligament, grows and builds itself up in love, as each part does its work."
Ephesians 4:16

The discipline of being a good team member is real work.

"Not looking to your own interests but each of you to the interest of the others."
Philippians 2:4

VOL 2 TEAMWORK

Saying to a teammate, "Let me help you," can go a long way in building an unbreakable bond.

"And do not forget to do good and to share with others, for with such sacrifices God is pleased."
Hebrews 13:16

THE PRAYING ATHLETE

Acknowledging those who help you makes others want to help you and your team.

"We always thank God for all of you
and continually mention you
in our prayers."
1 Thessalonians 1:2

_____
_____
_____
_____

Forgiveness opens new doors in team relationships.

"Be kind and compassionate to one another, forgiving each other, just as in Christ God forgave you."
Ephesians 4:32

Find two things you like about a team and let the teammates know. This will build unity and trust.

"Finally, brothers and sisters, rejoice! Strive for full restoration, encourage one another, be of one mind, live in peace. And the God of love and peace will be with you."
2 Corinthians 13:11

Be thankful that you are part of a team. You are part of something greater than yourself.

"Let the peace of Christ rule in your hearts, since as members of one body you were called to peace. And be thankful."
Colossians 3:15

Whether you like your team or not, embrace each other's differences.

"There are different kinds of gifts, but the same Spirit distributes them. There are different kinds of service, but the same Lord. There are different kinds of working but in all of them and in everyone it is the same God at work."
1 Corinthians 12:4-6

Say, "I'm committed to help build this team." Once voiced, it can come alive in your spirit, and the team can flourish.

"For the word of God is alive and active. Sharper than any double-edged sword, it penetrates even to the dividing soul and spirit, joints and marrow; it judges the thoughts and attitudes of the heart."
Hebrews 4:12

A good team will always say it loved its coach and each other. Breathe the right love language into your team.

"Above all, love each other deeply, because love covers over a multitude of sins."
1 Peter 4:8

Do not allow your teammates to turn you into a puppet. Instead, enable your teammates to show you how to grow, and hold on to your own identity.

"In fact, though by this time you ought to be teachers, you need someone to teach you the elementary truths of God's word all over again. You need milk, not solid food! Anyone who lives on milk, being still an infant, is not acquainted with the teaching about righteousness."
Hebrews 5:12-13

Build your team within your community. Serve together, walk together, laugh together, love each other, and together you will be forever remembered as a team that accomplished much. A team can bring hope to a community.

"Therefore, as God's chosen people, holy and dearly loved, clothe yourselves with compassion, kindness, humility, gentleness and patience. Bear with each other and forgive one another if any of you has a grievance against someone. Forgive as the Lord forgave you. And over all these virtues put on love, which binds them all together in perfect unity."
Colossians 3:12-14

If teammates and coaches focus on your bad traits, chances are you will be discouraged. However, you can focus on the good traits of your teammates and coaches. By encouraging one another, each person grows as a player and teammate.

"I myself am convinced, my brothers and sisters, that you yourselves are full of goodness, filled with knowledge and competent to instruct one another."
Romans 15:14

**Rise to the occasion as a unit,
instead of as an individual.**

"Let us therefore make every effort to
do what leads to peace
and to mutual edification."
Romans 14:19

Championships are for teams who listen to the same voice.

"Turning your ear to wisdom and applying your heart to understanding."
Proverbs 2:2

You cannot choose your teammates, but you can change their attitudes with encouragement and support.

"Now that you have purified yourselves by obeying the truth so that you have sincere love for each other, love one another deeply, from the heart."
1 Peter 1:22

To be a winner, surround yourself with winners.

"Walk with the wise and become wise,
for a companion of fools suffers harm."
Proverbs 13:20

THE PRAYING ATHLETE

Teach your team to play with the passion that fuels you.

"Then make my joy complete by being like-minded, having the same love, being one in spirit and of one mind."
Philippians 2:2

Maintain your value as a teammate by being present, diligent, and enduring the process, no matter the circumstance.

"Do your best to present yourself to God as one approved, a worker who does not need to be ashamed and who correctly handles the word of truth."
2 Timothy 2:15

Listen to the voices of your teammates. They might have something to teach you.

"Listen to advice and accept discipline, and at the end you will be counted among the wise."
Proverbs 19:20

_____
_____
_____
_____

What value can you bring to the team besides your physical skills?

"For physical training is of some value, but godliness has value for all things, holding promise for both the present life and the life to come."
1 Timothy 4:8

Would you want your teammates to play with your passion and energy?

"Being strengthened with all power according to his glorious might so that you may have great endurance and patience..."
Colossians 1:11

Teams need more troubleshooters and fewer troublemakers. The troubleshooters find ways to shut down the troublemakers, making room for unity and team chemistry. Be a troubleshooter!

"I appeal to you, brothers and sisters, in the name of our Lord Jesus Christ, that all of you agree with one another in what you say and that there be no divisions among you, but that you be perfectly united in mind and thought."
1 Corinthians 1:10

VOL 3
GROWTH & PREP. FOR THE FUTURE

Make the most of your time now. We all will be replaced at some point.

"Teach us to number our days, that we may gain a heart of wisdom."
Psalm 90:12

Getting stronger does not always mean physically, but rather mentally, emotionally, and spiritually.

"I pray that out of his glorious riches he may strengthen you with power through his Spirit in your inner being."
Ephesians 3:16

Habits are hard to develop and break. Make your good habits a thing of the present and future, and make your bad habits a thing of the past.

"If we confess our sins, he is faithful and just and will forgive us our sins and purify us from all unrighteousness."
1 John 1:9

Never allow minor challenges to sidetrack your mental focus, use the minor challenges to build the foundation of your mental strength.

"Consider it pure joy, my brothers and sisters, whenever you face trials of many kinds, because you know that the testing of your faith produces perseverance. Let perseverance finish its work so that you may be mature and complete, not lacking anything."
James 1:2-4

Doing the same things over and over again will result in a continuation of the past. If you don't want history to repeat itself, you have to adjust your game plan.

"Whatever you have learned or received or heard from me, or seen in me – put it into practice. And the God of peace will be with you."
Philippians 4:9

When you think the race is finished it is just beginning, one victory does not mean the race of life is completed. Keep pushing!

"Therefore, since we are surrounded by such a great cloud of witnesses, let us throw off everything that hinders and the sin that so easily entangles. And let us run with perseverance the race marked out for us."
Hebrews 12:1

What is the destination of your life? Draw a map and layout your plan and destination. You cannot get to where you want to go if you do not have a plan in mind. Plan ahead to arrive on time.

"In their hearts humans plan their course, but the Lord establishes their steps."
Proverbs 16:9

_____
_____
_____
_____

Those who define greatness achieve greatness. If you cannot define greatness for your life, you cannot find it. Define greatness for yourself and you will find and achieve greatness.

"You will increase my honor and comfort me once more."
Psalm 71:21

THE PRAYING ATHLETE

Courage is fear wrapped in the sweat of preparation.

"Be watchful, stand firm in the faith,
act like men, be strong."
1 Corinthians 16:13

Your mindset can counter any setback.

"Finally, brothers and sisters, whatever is true, whatever is noble, whatever is right, whatever is pure, whatever is lovely, whatever is admirable – if anything is excellent or praiseworthy – think about such things."
Philippians 4:8

THE PRAYING ATHLETE

Trophies all end up in the attic. Enjoy your achievements, but keep your focus on the future.

"Being confident of this, that he who began a good work in you will carry it on to completion until the day of Christ Jesus."
Philippians 1:6

Control your thoughts with a winning attitude.

"Do not conform to the pattern of this world, but be transformed by the renewing of your mind. Then you will be able to test and approve that God's will is – his good, pleasing and perfect will."
Romans 12:2

Life is 10% what happens to you and 90% how you respond to it.

"Slaves, in reverent fear of God submit yourselves to your masters, not only to those who are good and considerate, but also to those who are harsh."
1 Peter 2:18

What do you need to sacrifice to achieve your goals, dreams and vision for your life?

"Therefore, I urge you, brothers and sisters, in view of God's mercy, to offer your bodies as a living sacrifice, holy and pleasing to God – this is your true and proper worship.
Romans 12:1

Who are you coaching in life? We are all coaches in our own way. Remind yourself of that fact, and it will help you have greater impact on others.

"In the same way, let your light shine before others, that they may see your good deeds and glorify your Father in heaven."
Matthew 5:16

Before you weigh in, drop off your cares and burdens into God's grace. You will see your heart will be much lighter.

"Cast all your anxiety on him because he cares for you."
1 Peter 5:7

People always say I want to be this or that, but they are never willing to make the commitment and sacrifice to attain those goals.

"Commit your way to the Lord; trust in him and he will do this."
Psalm 37:5

Many people will say you cannot do it, few will say you can.

"Jesus looked at them and said, 'With man this is impossible, but with God all things are possible.'"
Matthew 19:26

Building your own success is much more important than someone handing you success.

"And observe what the Lord your God requires: Walk in obedience to him, and keep his decrees and commands, his laws and regulations, as written in the Law of Moses. Do this so that you may prosper in all you do and wherever you go."
1 Kings 2:3

Having a plan and implementing a plan are totally different. Take steps to implement your plan today.

"The plans of the diligent lead to profit as surely as haste leads to poverty."
Proverbs 21:5

Where you come from cannot hold you back from where you want to go, only you can.

"There is neither Jew nor Gentile, neither slave nor free, nor is there male and female, for you are all one in Christ Jesus."
Galatians 3:28

Extraordinary moments don't take place without extraordinary preparation along the way.

"Suppose one of you wants to build a tower. Won't you first sit down and estimate the cost to see if you have enough money to complete it?"
Luke 14:28

Chase the money and lose the dream; chase the dream, and the money will come to you.

"For the love of money is a root of all kinds of evil. Some people, eager for money, have wandered form the faith and pierced themselves with many griefs."
1 Timothy 6:10

What is behind me is done forever and cannot be changed. I am headed before me, toward my dreams and goals.

"Brothers and sisters, I do not consider myself yet to have taken hold of it. But one thing I do: Forgetting what is behind and straining toward what is ahead, I press on toward the goal to win the prize for which God has called me heavenward in Christ Jesus."
Philippians 3:13-14

Losses uncover your areas of need. Embrace them. Failure is a great teacher.

"But he said to me, 'My grace is sufficient for you, for my power is made perfect in weakness.' Therefore I will boast all the more gladly about my weaknesses, so that Christ's power may rest on me."
2 Corinthians 12:9

Every day, do something to take off and make your dreams happen. If you do nothing, nothing will happen. Take off today.

"Flee the evil desires of the youth and pursue righteousness, faith, love, and peace, along with those who call on the Lord out of a pure heart."
2 Timothy 2:22

When you feel like your hopes and dreams are fading away just hang on! That is a feeling not a fact!

"Not only so, but we also glory in our sufferings, because we know that suffering produces perseverance; perseverance, character; and character, hope."
Romans 5:3-4

Never let a day pass without taking a step toward your dreams. This is the only way they become reality.

"Strengthening the disciples and encouraging them to remain true to the faith. 'We must go through many hardships to enter the kingdom of God,' they said."
Acts 14:22

THE PRAYING ATHLETE

Breakaway from whatever it is that's keeping you from achieving your goals.

"If we confess our sins, he is faithful and just and will forgive us our sins and purify us from unrighteousness."
1 John 1:9

VOL 3 GROWTH & PREP.

They say good things come to those who wait. I say good things come to those who work.

"And with you, Lord, is unfailing love; and, You reward everyone according to what they have done."
Psalm 62:12

# VOL 4 KEEPING THE RIGHT MENTALITY

THE PRAYING ATHLETE

> Be confident, for today did not come by chance, but rather through the time and commitment to walk this journey of hard work and dedication to perfect the talents God gave you.

VOL 4 RIGHT MENTALITY

People don't know what it costs to be you. They don't know the sacrifices you made along the way. All they see is the smile on your face, because being you is cool when you know what it costs.

What joy! Go, my friend, in His confidence and claim the blessing that is ahead!

Respond believing you can and you will, knowing nothing can make you respond in a negative way because you have dreams and goals to achieve.

> Regret is a tough thing to live with. If you live life not wanting to live with regret, you will find yourself taking chances and living life to the fullest.

_____
_____
_____
_____

VOL 4 RIGHT MENTALITY

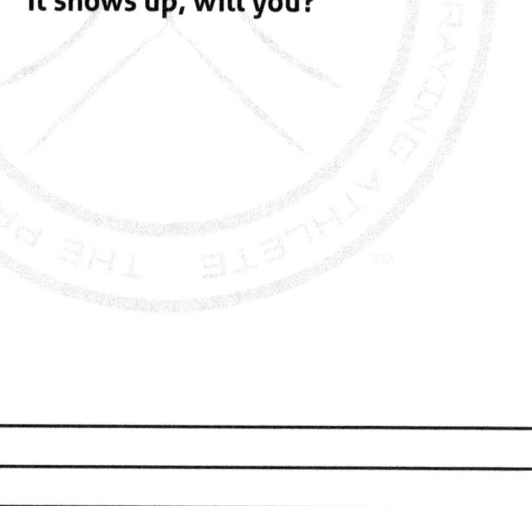

**Go get life every day.
It shows up, will you?**

_____
_____
_____
_____

The blessings of life ahead will allow you to impact people for me. Be confident in the tests I have ahead for you, embrace the rushing waters of life as I rush my goodness into your life. May you hear my voice as you hear the waters and may my spirit move and consume your life.

Always work on your negotiating skills. I get something free wherever I go. Just last night the restaurant was closing. I asked if there were any care packages as I go. She said no. I said, surely there is something.
She said yes, okay, and she brought me a big box of fresh baked cookies that had not been sold that day.
Asking is a key ingredient to some of the best things you ever taste.

When you give up, you may feel like life ripped you off. However, it is time to step up and step back into life.

VOL 4 RIGHT MENTALITY

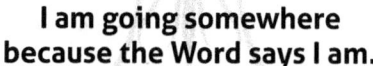

I am going somewhere because the Word says I am.

THE PRAYING ATHLETE

You want to be better, but at what price?

_____
_____
_____
_____

VOL 4 RIGHT MENTALITY

I may not be happy today, but I am content because I know and believe many good days are ahead, no matter what this day may hold.

THE PRAYING ATHLETE

We all want express success, but no success comes without pressing.

VOL 4 RIGHT MENTALITY

> Every day, rise with anticipation for the day you have been granted. Just breathe and feel the air in your lungs.

_____
_____
_____
_____

THE PRAYING ATHLETE

**Has adversity
discouraged you?
If so, say
"This will not conquer me.
This I shall overcome."**

VOL 4 RIGHT MENTALITY

It is the things that are
invisible that we worry about
99 percent of the time -
the unknown.
Live in the present, and you
will be confident 99 percent
of the time.

_____
_____
_____
_____

THE PRAYING ATHLETE

Control your thoughts with a winning attitude.

_____
_____
_____
_____

VOL 4 RIGHT MENTALITY

Embrace everything that happens, but do not consume everything that happens.

Prepare with the process in mind, but know the process before you prepare.

VOL 4 RIGHT MENTALITY

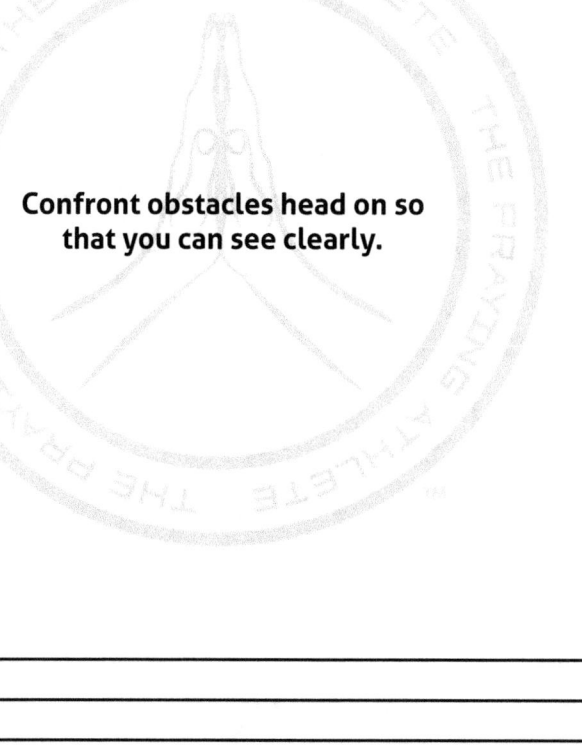

Confront obstacles head on so that you can see clearly.

THE PRAYING ATHLETE

Imagine where you want to go, then go.

**Do you want it?
Then EARN it with maximum effort during every waking moment of your life.
Why not?
You said you want it, right?
This is how you earn it!**

What makes a successful business person? It is simple: do things that others think are below them or mundane. The business person can see the need to do the task in order for others to be successful.

Take Charge! Live life focused on your lifetime, not the minutes and moments of life. If you make choices through the lens of your lifetime, and not the lens of the moment, it will enable you to take charge of your life and protect your heart from the painful choices you make in a moment of weakness. Find your strength by taking charge and guarding your heart.

The seemingly insignificant choices you make every day are determining whether or not you are fulfilling your destiny.

In life, if you only do what people ask, you won't last. Results and excellence are driven by the desire to achieve beyond what is asked.

Pray for the success of those you can impact with the success God grants you.

Ask your loved ones how you can show your love for them.

We all start to complain when we compare ourselves to others. Stop comparing and start sharing all the goodness you have to give away.

VOL 4 RIGHT MENTALITY

> **Yesterday is now gone, embrace this new day with an incredible sense of urgency to overcome any barriers that made yesterday or any day, a challenge.**

VOL 5 STAYING MOTIVATED

THE PRAYING ATHLETE

Today was gifted to you. Now choose what to do with the gift of today. You can put it away and not open the gift of today, or you can unwrap your day and put all your talents to use to make tomorrow an even better day.

VOL 5 STAYING MOTIVATED

Going places takes energy and progress every second to get to where you want to be. Always remember to keep pressing when it gets tough. You WILL get there.

**How do you get from good to great?
Push the good to the side and always focus on being great.
Greatness will arrive.**

_____
_____
_____
_____

VOL 5 STAYING MOTIVATED

**Are you a leader?
How do you know
if you have never defined
what a leader is?**

THE PRAYING ATHLETE

Go out and achieve the impossible.

VOL 5 STAYING MOTIVATED

I'm not finished with what God has challenged me to accomplish in my life.

Why sweat the moment when the One you know is there with you in the moment?

Do your circumstances intimidate you? Pray and let God give you the wisdom to be an overcomer!

**Do what you need to do to
dream again.
Fill the visions of your life and
dream on.**

VOL 5 STAYING MOTIVATED

In despair, there is hope around the corner.

THE PRAYING ATHLETE

Be that hope so that others can find it.

VOL 5 STAYING MOTIVATED

Building your own success is much more important than someone handing you success.

Today, do something to be something UNBELIEVABLE.

VOL 5 STAYING MOTIVATED

**You cannot become what you
need to be and what
God wants you to be if you
remain where you are.
Strive to do more.**

> What time is it in your life? Always be engaged in a season of growth, finding ways to study, read, and grow your circle of influence.

_____
_____
_____
_____

What is your ground speed?
How quickly do you pursue
your goals and plans?
A slow ground speed will not
take you anywhere fast.
It is a big world out there with
many goals to achieve.
Increase your ground
speed today.

THE PRAYING ATHLETE

Today is the first day of your new life. God created you and me to have a fresh start every day.

_____
_____
_____
_____

**The storms may gather and
the wind may blow but I know
the sun will always show
through the darkness of life.**

If you look closely, help is
always on the way.
Sometimes, it is hard to see,
but God always delivers.

New opportunities bring new ways to rise to the top of your career. So, the stress you feel is not real, but the enthusiasm for what is ahead is what keeps you on top.

_____
_____
_____
_____

THE PRAYING ATHLETE

Be on the front lines and lead.

VOL 5 STAYING MOTIVATED

People will try to wipe you away and discount who you are and say things that will hurt you. But stand tall and fly away to those you know care and love you.

THE PRAYING ATHLETE

Grab life and fill it with love, joy, peace and happiness.

God gave you a special talent to elevate Him and to bless you and your family. Through this gift he has given you, it will build a platform for a stronger and deeper faith as you rely on God and not yourself.
Now, embrace your talent. All the confidence is already within you, so ACTIVATE it!

THE PRAYING ATHLETE

Renewable energy is a hot topic today. How can you help others renew their interest, energy, and zeal for life?

Have you ever been on a balance beam? Have you seen the routines by some of the best during the Olympics? Balance in life is very challenging. Be prepared for the fall—it will happen. Even the best fall. It is the getting back up that requires the discipline and self-motivation to conquer any self-doubt. The victory is getting back up!

The tongue is such a powerful tool. Use it to give words of affirmation every day.

> Why do people drive slow in the fast lane? Step aside, and let us move. We are trying to make something happen.

THE PRAYING ATHLETE

> A goal in life should be to empower people and give away whatever knowledge you have to them.

_____
_____
_____
_____

So many times, we as athletes put undue pressure on our talents. When we do this, we play robotically and that limits our potential. Play with zeal and passion for the game you love, and you will leave anxiety behind. You will then surpass what was possible and begin reaching what others thought was impossible.

VOL 6 PERSONAL ACCOUNTABILITY

THE PRAYING ATHLETE

We live in a world today where cameras are everywhere. The eye in the sky does not lie. If we taped our lives for a week and went back and viewed the film, what would it say about us?

Accept your limitations in life, but put people in your life that can help you overcome your limitations, so you can embrace the expectation without limitation.

Be careful what your eyes see and ears hear. Once we take it in we cannot cast it away— it is always there. Our brain and eyes cannot dismiss what is captured. There is no eraser for the brain.

If you hurt someone, never be too stubborn to stop and say you are sorry.

If you were honest with yourself, what could you say to someone? It may open a whole new world for you.

Clients see your sacrifice, work, and availability to help them be successful. Never doubt someone is watching you.

> **To be aligned with your client means you must be totally committed to what is best for your client, not yourself.**

VOL 6 ACCOUNTABILITY

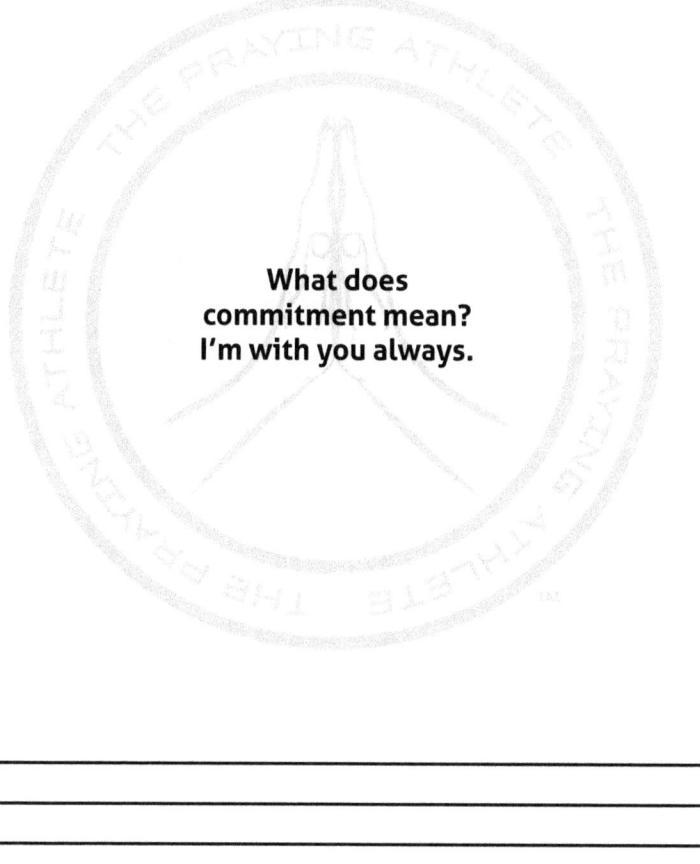

What does commitment mean? I'm with you always.

THE PRAYING ATHLETE

> People say, "I love you," but they never give back to the person they say they love. That is not love; that is selfishness.

Do not allow your mind to overtake your heart. You heart must win every time.

THE PRAYING ATHLETE

What will your teammates say about you 10 years from now?

_____
_____
_____
_____

What are you reading to help yourself become better at what you do?

_____
_____
_____
_____

THE PRAYING ATHLETE

Prepare with the process in mind, but know the process before you prepare.

_____
_____
_____
_____

VOL 6 ACCOUNTABILITY

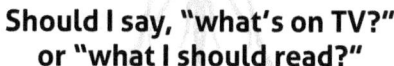

**Should I say, "what's on TV?"
or "what I should read?"**

_____
_____
_____
_____

THE PRAYING ATHLETE

> **I know where I want to go and how I want to get there, I'm just not sure who to take with me, or if they are ready.**

_____
_____
_____
_____

VOL 6 ACCOUNTABILITY

Social media robs you of so much. Stay away from it for one week, and watch your life excel in new ways.

When you love someone unconditionally it can be painful, but to put conditions on the love will bring regret.

> Not doing something for someone is a tough decision— sometimes it breaks your heart. But, your choice not to may be the new energy they need to do for themselves. This is how you can grow your relationship and make it go deeper and more refined.

Your heart aches for someone you love when you know you cannot fix what ails them. They have to choose to fix themselves; that cannot be your job. If you try, it will only strain the relationship.

VOL 6 ACCOUNTABILITY

Choices can be simple in life. The right choice, however, requires diligence and personal commitment to finding the right ingredients for that choice.

I wonder how many people have said, "If I never took that step, what could I have become?" No need to wonder; the answer is millions and millions. People will tempt you with one drink, one smoke of weed, one snort of cocaine or whatever it maybe. They will say things like, "this will never hurt anybody," or "go ahead, try it, have some fun and hang out." Choose today not to be a statistic, but to make choices that will help you standout and not put your life on standby.

_____
_____
_____
_____

A coach cannot fix what you fake. It is time to make yourself better, finish the race, embrace the process, complete the task. Now, ask the coach to shape you and mold you into the athlete he believes you can be. When you humble yourself and ask for help, the growth you truly desire will begin to flow into your life and skill set.

THE PRAYING ATHLETE

If someone implanted you with a GPS unbeknown to you and they were able to track you, what would they find out about you that they do not know today?

VOL 6 ACCOUNTABILITY

You can control your choices.
No need to derail your life
and career with poor choices.
Make smart choices.

Why does laziness keep you from achieving success? Maybe you need to first define laziness. One definition of laziness is to steal away time and energy from things that can produce success into one's life. Internet, TV, social media, and over-sleeping can cause laziness.
What are your four?

_____
_____
_____
_____

VOL 6 ACCOUNTABILITY

Think about something in your life. Now ask yourself, will this one thing help guide me to my goals and plans? If so, embrace it with the upmost energy. If not, cut it off and let it fly far far away.

THE PRAYING ATHLETE

You can build all types of items with Legos. The Lego pattern, if followed, can build some incredible things. Think about what the patterns are in your life and will the current patterns help you achieve your dreams. If not, start some new patterns.

_____
_____
_____
_____

Life sometimes can seem very lonely, dark and feel as though you are the only one battling life's challenges and the curves during the journey. Always look for the signs along the way to tell you what may be ahead. It will prevent you from crashing.

THE PRAYING ATHLETE

You can control your LEGACY, CHOICES, and JOURNEY with the people you allow to be a part of your story.

_____
_____
_____
_____

May God use my hands and feet today to captivate an eye or an ear. May that eye and ear hear the talent that could only be God-given. May they begin to know God through my life, and may God use this talent to begin a journey for those who do not know the God of the Bible.

VOL 7 LIVING LIFE
PART 1

THE PRAYING ATHLETE

I know the progress will be tough and may be lonely at times as I find new friends and people to help me. But this I do know, I must make the changes in my life because I cannot survive just being ordinary when I know I was created to be extraordinary. I will make progress every day from now on and promise myself not to allow my past or laziness to paralyze my future. I will be this person of change. I must be the person of change. It starts now, today!

_____
_____
_____
_____

As you step out into your new day and your new start, keep this in mind: Anything and everything that has ever been accomplished at one time or another was new. For you see, the newness of each day is another start toward where you desire to go. So, embrace this day beginning with a fresh dose of energy. It is just another step toward the hope that is within your soul. Keep stepping and you will arrive to the DESTINATION and GOAL of YOUR choice. Meanwhile, continue to gather, grow and challenge your talents daily.

_____
_____
_____
_____

Read more, attend church, get around people that can help you grow. Spend more time thinking about the future and mapping it out and less about what happened in the past. Find the motivation to read and listen to things that build into you as a person. Sleep less and exercise your brain and your physical body.

Educate = Read More
Empower = Believe More
Elevate = Achieve More

People will try to wipe you away, discount who you are, and say things that will hurt you. But, stand tall and fly away to those you know care and love you.

VOL 7 LIVING LIFE PT. 1

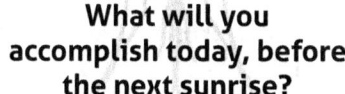

What will you accomplish today, before the next sunrise?

_____
_____
_____
_____

THE PRAYING ATHLETE

> We all add value into each other's lives by getting to know each other more and more, and by giving and not taking. For you see, this is not the world's love you see on TV. This is true love that can only be found by opening one's heart to another and being yourself...finding the joy in the journey together, no matter how long or hard.

_____
_____
_____
_____

VOL 7 LIVING LIFE PT. 1

You are loved when you are born. You will be loved when you die. In between, YOU have to manage!!!

We are always in motion!
The ocean moves every day.
The waves come to the
shoreline 24/7.
There is purpose in the
ocean's motion.
Does your motion
have purpose?
If so, what is the purpose?
Make your motion count every
day, just like the ocean!

_____
_____
_____
_____

VOL 7 LIVING LIFE PT. 1

In our lives, we can chase and fill our time with the pursuit of material things. While doing this, we can easily lose sight of what we do have and the blessings of today. As you strive for excellence, always maintain The Thankful Heart. It will certainly project you and give back great rewards to you and your talents.

_____
_____
_____
_____

THE PRAYING ATHLETE

It is your passion that will overtake the competition. It is your passion that will not allow yourself to set an artificial ceiling of growth and success. Your passion will take you beyond what you thought was possible and delete the word impossible from your vocabulary.
Live life with
AMAZING PASSION.

_____
_____
_____
_____

Time is of the essence.
I must maintain my focus.
My strong will has carried me.
It is about to happen.
I will chain myself daily to
purpose and passion.
I will follow my heart.
I cannot be deterred.
Doubters will soon see.
I believe.
IT WILL HAPPEN.

THE PRAYING ATHLETE

Sometimes we have to dig deep to take out the problems we put into our own life.

VOL 7 LIVING LIFE PT. 1

**The Blessing awaits.
Always remember God will
release you to bless you.**

> Finding the wow factor in life can be as simple as releasing something to find the something that God has for you.

Where is your power coming from? Try this. Tap into the power of the one that created you. His power is endless and bountiful.

The pain of a breakup, no matter what it may be, can be intense and misunderstood. Pain is actually the first step to healing. We cannot heal if we never embrace the pain and hurt. Jesus experienced the greatest hurt and his healing was marvelous. It brought a new life and new body. So as much as it hurts, know it is better to go through the pain than to live in the pain and hurt for an entire life. The healing may seem long, but in the scope of life it is very short. So remember, the pain is actually healing masked.

**Preparing for your success of tomorrow will be tougher than you think or realize. That is why only a few will make it to the other side.
Will it be you?
Do your part daily and make choices that will carry you to the other side! Know that your competition will eliminate itself. Many will lack the endurance to finish. Let that never be said of you. Go now and set out to compete daily, finish and finish strong.**

THE PRAYING ATHLETE

> Finding hope can be a
> challenge in this world.
> Instead of searching for the
> hope you need, give hope to
> others and the hope you
> desire will find you at the
> doorsteps of your life.

_____
_____
_____
_____

**Give what you want:
Give Love, Get Love.
Give Hope, Get Hope.
Give Friendship, Get a Friend.
Give Time, Get Time.
Give Resources,
Get Resources.
Give Help, Get Help.
Give into Relationships,
Get Positive Relationships.
Give into Fitness, Get Fit.**

Live your life for you, your family, and to honor God. What others think or believe is irrelevant. Once you believe this and engage in this thought, you will be free from what others do or think. Instead of saying, "Look at how much fun they are having.", you will say, "I'm glad they could that".
The freedom that comes with enjoying your minutes and seizing your time will free your spirit to enjoy life as it was meant to be. We will be simple and satisfied with ourselves, and willing to serve others rather than ourselves.

The difference in between two things is called a gap. I have started something called The Gap Principal. Here are some examples: The difference in between wanting to be a professional athlete and being a professional athlete, or wanting to be successful in whatever field and being successful, is a gap. It is what happens between the gaps that allows for success. If we do not fill this gap, we will always stay in the want stage while life passes by. Fill the gap if you really want it.

_____

_____

_____

_____

In this life, some will try to discourage you and say you cannot accomplish the goals and plans that are within your heart. No matter what your personal circumstances or challenges, make the adjustments.

We walk around life in a state of paralysis because we cannot let go of our past. Letting go of the past is the first step to find the hope that is ahead. Our future cannot be embraced if we continue to fall and get pulled back into the past.

Others will deplete your dream and strip away your belief, but be prayerful and you can connect yourself with people you add value to your life. You may have to search for that person, but that special connection will sustain you during the storms of life.

Every day you must purchase perseverance, patience, honesty, endurance, truthfulness, determination and focus.

THE PRAYING ATHLETE

Remember on this day and everyday that you are precious and beautiful, inside and out. Once God delivers His perfect blessing, you will be forever respected and cherished than ever before.

_____
_____
_____
_____

Today choose this:
Give thanks for your job!
Give thanks for the resources
you receive from your job!
Give thanks for the health you
have to do your job!
Give thanks for the people
that make you better
at your job! The challenges
you have in your job will now
be released, because you have
given thanks for all things
related to your job.

Finding true love is tougher than finding a needle in a haystack. However, it can be found. Be patient, and do not settle for less when God has more.

Sometimes, we need to remember where we were and the state of yesterday to enjoy our new day. This will push our confidence to capture what is ahead.

_____
_____
_____
_____

VOL 8
LIVING LIFE
PART 2

THE PRAYING ATHLETE

Relationships are so much like the ocean: back and forth, the waves cleaning as they go. Always be willing to give and take with each other along the way.

Fans cool us off in the heat. Sometimes we just need to be quiet and stop producing so much hot air.

THE PRAYING ATHLETE

What are you transporting in your life that can be dropped off to help someone in his or her own life?

_____
_____
_____
_____

VOL 8 LIVING LIFE PT. 2

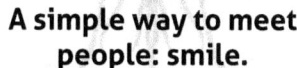

A simple way to meet people: smile.

**Do you want a
better solution?
Simple.
You speak, I listen,
I speak, you listen.**

If you have to choose between right and wrong you must first define the right and wrong in your life and have a guide. Allow the Bible to be your guide.

THE PRAYING ATHLETE

Have you ever noticed how corn is planted so closely together? Unless it is planted closely together, the corn cannot grow. Each stalk helps the next stalk grow as they protect each other from storms. Stay close to others and protect each other from the storms of life.

How do you know if you love someone? Pray for them, think about them, honor and respect them, trust them, and believe in them.

Finding freedom from past relationships is no easy task. The freedom you are looking for may not be possible because you cannot let go.

Building momentum in a relationship requires energy by both parties.

THE PRAYING ATHLETE

What are you pressing toward? It could be greatness or sadness. Two different roads, but both you can press. Choose your road today.

_____
_____
_____
_____

VOL 8 LIVING LIFE PT. 2

Our life is made up of seasons: good, bad, and some sad. But, we all can protect the time we have now and prepare to be better for those tough times ahead.

THE PRAYING ATHLETE

As a leader, you can steer the conversation. If you want to be better, steer it better.

VOL 8 LIVING LIFE PT. 2

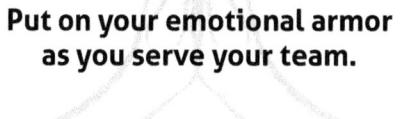

Put on your emotional armor as you serve your team.

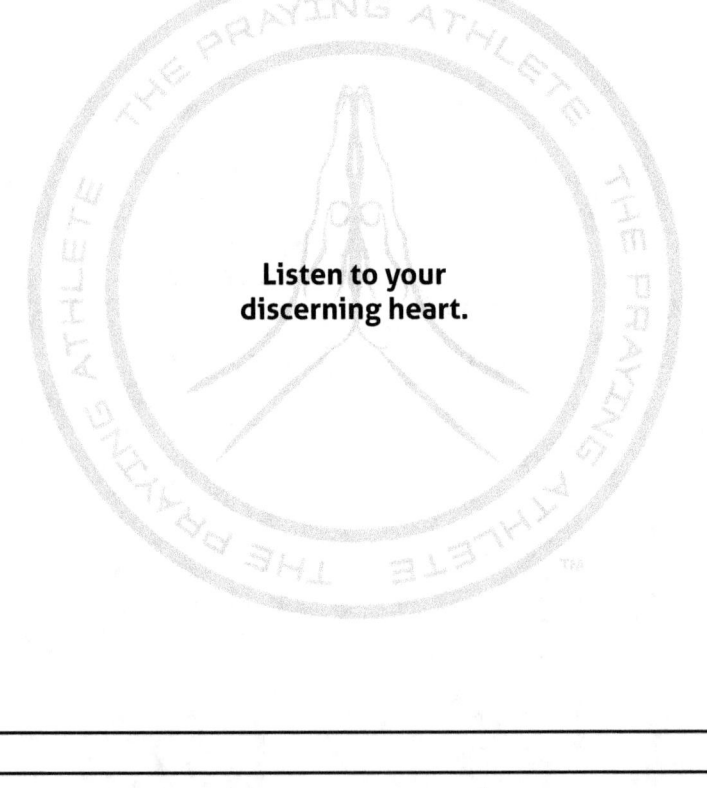

Listen to your discerning heart.

**Hug more, embrace more,
say thank you more.
Give more to find more.**

Have you ever missed the road sign? Missed your turn? The sign is there to help us. What signs are we missing in our own lives to enable us to get back on the right path?

_____
_____
_____
_____

VOL 8 LIVING LIFE PT. 2

Find a way to give back to those who have given to you. It can be big or small— maybe just a card to say, "I appreciate you more than words could ever say or explain, and you mean the world to me." That is a great start. It gets tiresome when just one side is doing all the giving. Everyone can give something. You can give your words, presence or time. And that could be worth more than any monetary gift to some, because there is no value for that.

_____
_____
_____
_____

THE PRAYING ATHLETE

Lighthouses help people and boats find their way. Be a lighthouse for someone today.

Instead of crying about what you do not have, take time to go give something to someone who does not have.

THE PRAYING ATHLETE

When you have a passion to chase after God, you will find yourself doing and acting with more zeal and focus than others, and that is okay. They will either catch up with you one day or new people will come into your life to continue to push you on this journey.

_____
_____
_____
_____

Sometimes we need to accelerate to get to our next goal. Sometimes we need to park and get some rest. There are times we need to look back at God's blessing and goodness. And, there are times we need to let go and make sure God is guiding us. So, we put our lives in neutral and do not press on. However, to do any of the above for an extended time will cause us to lose our way. Find the balance you need in your life, and embrace each phase as a way to endure the race of life.

THE PRAYING ATHLETE

> At one time, the fax machine was an incredible breakthrough in technology. Now, it is almost totally obsolete. Always change and update your skills to meet the needs of tomorrow.

VOL 8 LIVING LIFE PT. 2

How can you decide what you want to be if you have not decided what you can be with God's help.
You cannot do it alone.

Friends can be a hindrance or a blessing. Some friends never want you to succeed, so they will try to discourage you in their own manipulative way. Find the friends who will give you good counsel with no benefit for themselves, and you will find a friend for life.

Umbrellas have so many purposes. It protects us from rain, wind, hail, snow, ice, and even the sun. But it symbolizes much more than that. It is a shelter in the tough times and a place of refuge. Keep your spiritual umbrella, the word of God, close by.
The storms of life are coming.

To be great you must believe in yourself. You must have a drive, be focused, be confident and grab all your energy to overcome the negative noise of the day. But the real, true key is to be so competitive that you rise up early to beat the birds to make the first beautiful sound of the day.

_____
_____
_____
_____

When you promise yourself something and you focus your efforts on attaining your promise, one thing to remember is the process to achieve the promise will be always be a challenge. The promise you made cannot be achieved without pushing through your personal process. Everyone's process is different but one thing we know is that it will not be easy to achieve your promise without a journey full of processes. Buckle up!

_____
_____
_____
_____

If you have it within your sphere of influence to do good through encouragement, a helping hand, serving or giving, what should you do? Worry about how you may be perceived? Be concerned what someone may say? No! Do it! Changing a person's life is more important than anything you can accomplish. One small deed could give someone the will to push for another day, so DO IT.

Have faith my friend. He will deliver in His time. Allow Him to do His work and be careful not to circumvent His work with your work and your plans. Be patient. His work and timing will be much more beautiful than anything you can imagine or dream of, but you must first subject your will to His will. The first step is to engage faith. Make it real and purposeful in your life. When He does release you, oh...hold on! Your heart will be overwhelmed with such joy, peace, and total fulfillment, because the journey He has you on is the journey He wants to fulfill in your life.
So, what's your next move? Just have faith.

_____
_____
_____
_____

THOUGHTS & REFLECTIONS

MY QUOTES

ACKNOWLEDGMENTS

I want to acknowledge and say thank you to all those that helped with this project:

Nadia Guy
Ashlyn Helms
My Mom & Dad

All of my NFL Clients, current and former, that have encouraged me to share these words with others.

ABOUT
TPA

The Praying Athlete is a movement that creates an organic culture of prayer through an uplifting community and authentic conversation.

For more information, visit our website **www.theprayingathlete.com**.

Follow us on social media.

 @ThePrayingAthlete

 @Praying_Athlete

 @ThePrayingAthlete

COLLECT ALL
8 VOL.

Our first volume of *The Praying Athlete Quote Book* addresses the topic of playing the game. Quotes and thoughts from Robert B. Walker, paired with Scripture from God's Word, allow readers to get a good idea about what playing a good game looks like.

Our second volume of *The Praying Athlete Quote Book* addresses the topic of teamwork. Quotes and thoughts from Robert B. Walker, paired with Scripture from God's Word, allow readers to understand what it means to be a good teammate and surround yourself with people who lift you up.

Our third volume of *The Praying Athlete Quote Book* addresses the topic of growth & preparation for the future. Quotes and thoughts from Robert B. Walker, paired with Scripture from God's Word, allow readers to know that even though the future is uncertain, there is a plan and purpose for everyone.

Our fourth volume of *The Praying Athlete Quote Book* addresses the topic of keeping the right mentality. Quotes and thoughts from Robert B. Walker allow readers to understand how staying in the right mindset can improve overall performance.

 Our fifth volume of *The Praying Athlete Quote Book* addresses the topic of staying motivated. Quotes and thoughts from Robert B. Walker allow readers to become motivated to accomplish their goals, even when they feel they are not up to the task.

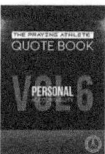 Our sixth volume of *The Praying Athlete Quote Book* addresses the topic of personal accountability. Quotes and thoughts from Robert B. Walker allow readers to think about how they can better themselves. Whether it is ending a bad habit or saying no to anything that may hurt themselves or others, staying accountable will benefit one's character and performance.

 Our seventh volume of *The Praying Athlete Quote Book* addresses the topic of living life. This volume is the first part in a two part living life series. Quotes and thoughts from Robert B. Walker give readers a better understanding of how to live life to the fullest.

 Our eighth volume of *The Praying Athlete Quote Book* addresses the topic of living life. This volume is the second part in a two part living life series. Quotes and thoughts from Robert B. Walker give readers a better understanding of how to live life to the fullest.

FOR MORE INFO AND MERCHANDISE, PLEASE VISIT
WWW.THEPRAYINGATHLETE.COM

CHECK OUT OUR
THE PRAYING ATHLETE™
PHOTOGRAPHY
QUOTE BOOKS

VOL. 1

VOL. 2

VOL. 3

VOL. 4

*The Praying Athlete Photography Quote Book*s celebrate God's glory and magnificence through His creation. They contain photos taken by Robert B. Walker, paired with his words of wisdom, motivation, and inspiration.

FOR MORE INFO AND MERCHANDISE, PLEASE VISIT
WWW.THEPRAYINGATHLETE.COM

www.ingramcontent.com/pod-product-compliance
Lightning Source LLC
LaVergne TN
LVHW051545070426
835507LV00021B/2417